Rasping Melodies: Painspirations of My Past

Roeau Vetrano

PandaMonk
PUBLISHING

ISBN-13: 978-0990517689
ISBN-10: 0990517683
PandaMonk Publishing, LLC
Alexandria, Virginia

I would like to dedicate this book to my loving parents, Malorie and Don, and my siblings, Siobahn and Tyrone, for being so open minded, accepting and supporting me every step in whatever direction I have taken in my life. You were the ones who were always there; never flinching, always positive and had my back when I came to you in need. I would like to acknowledge those who took pleasure in bringing me pain, tears and nightmares on a regular basis throughout my life. Thanks to you, I learned a very valuable and hard lesson on how to stand up and speak up for myself. Most of all, no matter how nasty it got, you shown me a prime example of the type of person I never wanted to become. I would also like to dedicate this work to Carole Joranlien-Prior that, through one sentence, opened a floodgate of pure potential that I never thought I had. You were the catalyst that set the ball in motion of my own self discovery. Deep in my heart, I am grateful and I will never forget it. I also want to pay respect to Debra F. Sosa. Through you, you have taught me how to fully accept all of myself and helped me find my voice. Most of all, I dedicate this book to my husband, Joey "Kujo" Jones. You are the only one I know who was able to vanquish the demons that I have been battling for years. Because of you, I am stronger than I have ever been. Because of you, I feel I am capable of doing anything. You are my life. You are my heart.

Table of Contents

Rasping Melodies: Painspirations of My Past

LGBT

Shunned.

Different.

Weird.

Freaky.

Nasty.

That awkward barrier you feel

most people don't tackle every day

holding back that percentage of you

until you are surrounded by accepting company.

We ALL have been there.

Even when we don't understand

each other's

intricate

delicate

way of living.

No matter our origin,

orientation

or lifestyle.

We ALL identify with one thought, one feeling;
lost,
uncertainty,
never truly figuring it out.

Then a light flickers
we venture forward towards that shining light
more understanding
more clarity.

Realizing
what has been natural to you
since day one is not meant to be,
when you step outside your door.

We are on the same journey
same path
same confusing struggle
no longer venturing it alone
accepting one another
embracing one another.

Truth

feeling whole

complete.

It becomes clear

knowing who you are.

Hesitation

A woman approaches a gentleman as he stands before a building that is engulfed in flames.
With his head tilted to the side, he strokes his chin, almost contemplating as he stares into the giant, licking bonfire.

The woman looks at the burning building then back at the man.

"The fire department in there?"

"Oh no," he says casually, continuing to watch.

"They're not!?" the woman replies, alarmed, "Then we gotta do something!" she announces, frantically rearing for action.

"Oh, I'm sure they're on their way. Almost every building has smoke detectors, now." he informs, half-heartedly dismissing the woman's urgency.

"Not EVERY place has smoke detectors and I don't hear any sirens!!!!" the woman retorts in a panic.

"Why would I go in there? I'm not a trained professional, and fire is hot," he says sarcastically. "I could run the risk of getting burned or dying. Besides, we don't know if there's anyone TO save in there," the man explains, justifying his lack of action as the sound of a little girl's voice pierces through the sound of a crackling, crumbling abode.

The woman's head whips back to the house.
"Oh my god," she whispers, without thinking of anything but to react.

She looks around the place to see a nearby ditch. She has nothing to cover herself with so she dives into the murky water, dousing herself before charging into the fiery box.

The apathetic man tilts his head to the other side as the woman ducks and disappears into the building.

1 minute passes.

2 minutes.

Then 3.

All that is heard is the crackling of the intense fire and the rumble of the crumbling house as it slowly falls apart.

A few minutes later, the woman comes charging out of the burning home with something swaddled within her arms. She stumbles forward, almost falling but catches herself as she tries to catch her breath. Gently setting the unconscious child on the ground, the woman remains on her hands and knees, coughing up a storm before collapsing on the ground, hacking and wheezing.

The man looks down at her, slowly shaking his head.

"What an idiot."

Wretched Throne

Shackled to an elegant extravagant chair,
the scalp of "The Regal" punctured by the sharp edges
of a crown
while the masses circle, awaiting the next direction.

"You're not listening to me!" the regal exclaims,
fidgeting and fighting to get free of the restraints.

"You can govern your own lives! Why does it always
have to be my word?" the regal asks,
a prisoner of power.

"Yes, but you would know better?" one commoner asks.
"What if something bad happens?" another chimes in.
"We are simply not smart enough," a third adds, starting
a domino effect.

"Not strong enough!"
"Not experienced enough!"
"Not attractive enough, popular enough, fast enough, fit
enough, rich enough!"

"Besides, It's scary out there!" an anonymous voice starts another tidal wave.

"It's too hot!"
"Too cold!"
"Too crowded!"
"Too empty!"
"Too familiar!"
"Too different!"
"Too inconvenient!"
"Too uncomfortable!...just don't want to."

The regal flinches at the tail end of the last sentence, turning palms up, shackles clinking.

"So this is it?" the regal asks, "THIS is what life is; a timeline of challenges. EVERY new experience is going to be scary, uncomfortable, inconvenient and awkward. It's ALWAYS been like that."

The masses expressions stay the same.

The regal, exhausted.

"This is how it's going to be? If something is going to be said, I am required to say it? If something is to be done, it is I that is expected to do it? And if I refuse to take action, I have failed you all? Where, if I try and I fail, I am the only one to blame, is that correct?"
the regal asks as the congregation slowly turns their faces away.

GGGGRRRRAAAAAHHHHHH!!!!!!!!

The regal roars; ripping, clawing and tearing at the chains.

Glass Case

Surrounded in all directions
by a two-way glass,
you can see everyone
but no one can see you.

Able to form opinions,
about everything and
everyone you see from a distance.

Dishing out and dishing out
throwing stones left and right
but forever stuck
in permanent "retreat" to avoid receiving
what you have been giving.

Well, you know what they say about people in glass
houses.

You think you can control everything,

every BAD thing around you but you can't,

not if you want good

great

or WONDERFUL in your life.

No "half-way

no "middle of the road"

no "on the fence"

or "compromise"

when it comes to REAL living

and 100% happiness.

You're either ALL in,

taking a leap of faith

of trust

and risk

or your half-assed version

of life

is depriving you

of what COULD be.

You either DO or you DON'T.

There is no third direction or option.

That "third direction" that you THINK is a choice

or a "new way of thinking"

is just a way to avoid something that you DON'T want to do.

Don't be afraid to

take responsibility

for your thoughts

for your feelings

for your words and actions

OWN yourself

and who you are inside.

Take charge of your own life

it is yours and ONLY yours.

"I think this and I feel that but don't look at me or react to what I say or do!"

NO!

I feel THIS way

I THINK this way

I TALK this way

ACT this way

and I will stand up before anyone who reacts

because I embrace EVERYTHING that I am.

I will not waver because I have no second thoughts or doubts or hesitations of who I am.

Unless I retract it myself

whatever I said

did

thought

or felt

is sticking.

Ghost

Merely a vessel.

Contents within scraped clean.

Discarded, empty, hollow and yet . . . not.

Existing, belonging and yet not.

Beyond fed up and tired, although not weary.

Continuing to walk this earthly realm.

Full of rage, sadness, pain and numb all at once.

Wracked.

Lifeless.

Beating to the heart of the earth.

Trapped in emotional,

carnal limbo.

Forever shall you walk between the cracks.

Acknowledged and altogether forgotten.

Heard and felt but disappearing in a wisp.

Retched

tortured

tainted

corrupted

lost soul.

Longing to be heard,

understood,

embraced.

And that long-standing weight

to be lifted from your shoulders.

So that you may, once, feel whole and complete again.

Whatever YOU say

I'm not gonna clarify
what you assume
Cuz to tell you the truth would just leave you more
room
to believe all the stories.
Trust all the gory
things people say simply out of their boredom
so believe what you see
in your head, cuz it's juicy.

Cuz I know it's not of the truth you are seeking
So YES, I'm a player
YES, I'm unfaithful
illegitimate son with the drugs on the table
Yes, I'll drink 'til I pass out
wake in a new bed
shoot up and snort up 'til I'm nearly half dead
drinkin' and smoke til I'm practically numb.

Then I'm hitting the road just to have some more fun

I got me a husband

got me a boyfriend

got every gurl say I'm welcome to come in.

I cut and I bleed

suicide several times

just can't kick these addictions that I'm calling life.

With a gun 'neath my head

extra clip by the bed

trust no one,

so I lie just so I'll keep a friend

Yes, I could try to clarify all of these things

or just be fucking thankful for every day

send a kiss to the heavens and thank God up above

cuz I know that he's carrying all of my love.

So keep spinning your webs and keep trying to top them

cuz there's one thing for sure that you're not gonna stop me

gonna keep moving forward, trudging day after day.

I don't care man

I'm just whatever you say

F*@ & You

The size of my ass is not your concern.
Nor are the size of my tits.
What I wear
what I do with my hair
whether or not I wear makeup.

What I decide to put on or in my skin
as well as whatever I decide to put in my body
be it drugs, alcohol or disgusting food
is also none of your business.

It never really mattered what I did with my life.
You would always find something "wrong" with it.
I should be somewhere other than where I am now.
I should say something other than what I said
or think in a different perspective than I already do.

You always know what's "right."
Well, you know what?

I never even considered your thoughts about my
choices.

Never asked.

Never cared.

Stop trying to "help" me

I didn't have a "problem" to begin with.

...You know what?...

What hurts the most is NOT the numerous people crushing down
upon me...

It's the select few special people who think and act just like them.

Wacko

Of course I love you.
But leave me alone
and watch me live life
as if you weren't home.

Don't touch me
don't talk to me
just listen to what I say.

Do whatever you want
but don't get in my way
watch me do this
and watch me do that.

Praise me
don't judge me
at the drop of a hat

But I can judge you of course,
because I am right.

Where would you be if I hadn't shown you the light?
I don't really need you
I said so myself
I merely want you here
to fill a void for myself.

I'm not interested in what you think or feel or what
you're into.

Be fascinated in everything I do
but I don't have to pay attention to you.
Oh sure!
I pay attention to all the flaws in your interests and ways of life.

If you only just listen to me you will see that I'm always right
don't ever text me while I'm busy
don't ever talk to me while I'm home

Okay, you can talk but nothing important.

And what is with all this wanting to kiss and hug?

And wanting to WHAT!?

Slow down, you nympho!

Twice a month is enough!

Sure, you can talk but not about your feelings

or me or "us."

It's really much better to sweep it under the rug.

You can say what you want

as long as you don't say it "this way"or "that"

say what you want AND the way that I want it.

BUT I won't tell you the right way until after you have spoken

Stop crying STOP CRYING!

SHUT THE FUCK UP! SHUT THE FUCK UP!!!!

YOU MANIPULATING BITCH!!!!

YOU'RE ONLY ACTING THIS WAY TO MAKE ME FEEL
BAD!!

YOU CAN DO WHATEVER YOU WANT!!
Under my approval.

If you just "got with the program" we could be great
together.

Leave me alone
don't talk to me, unless it's about fun or happy things
don't touch me
don't ask to spend time with me because I'm too busy
anticipating success
my image
money
things.

And quality time with others
I only believe in "cool" things
a flattering image and acceptance
so this "unconditional" thing you're looking for
I don't believe you'll ever find it
If you would just wake up to realize
that I'm the best you will ever have.

We'll get married and have kids

Just like I had planned

Disorder-ly Conduct

We all have our baggage.
So do I.

You need understanding?
You've got understanding.
But what is "understanding" to you?
Sure, I will put myself in your shoes
in your heart
in your mind
and understand
that you are dealing with an unexplainable
painful moment.

I will walk away

or come forward when I think it is best.

But do not take me for a psychic

do not take me for an errand boy

and do not think because you have a "problem"

that you have an all access pass to be an asshole

or treat me like shit.

You are hindered

but you are not crippled.

When I have a scary

hurtful

or painful thing holding me back

I study it

so I can conquer it and become stronger.

Oh I am not healing fast enough for you?
Fuck you!
At least I am taking strides to heal myself
rather than let the darkness within speak for me
and control me
YOU are your only problem
not me
YOU are the only reason
Why you THINK you know what I (and others) think,
feel and say about you.
Stop telling me what I think
stop telling me what I feel.

Of all the time we have known each other
You STILL truly do not know me
YOU are the only thing standing between you
and real happiness with the ones you care about
stop jabbing that index finger at others
because it should be aimed right between your eyes.
I "understand" it may be hard to admit
that you are the cause for your own pain
but you know what they say
admitting is the first step.

Joke

You wonder why I listen with a sideways glance.

When you know I've already given more than a second chance.

Don't you act all innocent and coy with me.

Your only motive is to toy with me.

I'm TRYING to be trusting.

Don't u take me for naive.

28 years on this earth.

You didn't "discover" me.

You put me on a pedestal just to drag me below your feet.

My only value to you is in between your sheets.

"Oh but I'M so much more different than every-" YEAH RIGHT

As soon as you find I won't undress, you end up taking flight.

Just save all of your promises and your stupid guarantees.

I know that your contract comes with hidden fees.

How can I trust that "this time will be the last time"?

When you have no control in violating what's mine?

You can tell me you are genuine but I know you are full of shit.

So, go sell your product elsewhere, I am not buying it.

Really?

You love me.

Really?

You want this for the rest of your life?

When everything I am

everything I say

everything I like

everything I do

feel

think

is pulled apart

and passed under a microscope

analyzed

and criticized

then edited for your contentment

passed thru filter after filter

until there is not much of "me" left.

So tell me again

what is it about me that you cannot live without?

Every action

every word

is being pre-screened before being carried out

because you're too sensitive to handle the real me.

Everything watered down

or cut out entirely

so you can enjoy your life in the spotlight

and all the glory of "you."

I keep my lips shut and stay agreeable

and make sure I don't push a wrong button

unfortunately, there are so many.

Oh, I can have fun and I can be happy

as long as it's approved by you or created by you.

I don't share my thoughts anymore
they're either stupid, silly, ridiculous, too strange
or you're flying off in rage, ready to fight
you always wonder why I do like something
and wonder why I don't
trying to convince me why something is good
or why what I like isn't.

Nothing is ever right the way it is
it's always worth contradicting
you're never happy with anything
never accepting of anything.

You've inherited his traits
and I don't see why I deserve to be
constantly punished
for your jealousies and insecurities.

Now that I'm pulled apart
edited
and watered down
until there is nothing much of "me" left
please tell me, what is it about me could you possibly want?

What could you possibly need?

Imagine me without a face and tell me.

How I look is not enough to keep me around.
What I do for YOU and how I make YOU feel is not
enough
what is it about ME that you could possibly want for all
eternity?

I'm tired of your major motivation being about you
or eventually it coming around to you
it seems that you won't get involved or bother
unless it affects you in some way.

So please tell me
is there room for me?
will we ever be equals?
will I ever be accepted
for who I am?

Or are you forever going to remain in the spotlight
as you leave me in the dust-filled darkness
expecting me to applaud you
silently watching you enjoy yourself
as I yearn for my moment of freedom and happiness?

If I have to TELL you to treat me with respect
equality, fairness, honesty, love and compassion
where is the meaning in that?

I've come to the conclusion
from all the games
that I am completely numb now.

Not a word nor action feels real now
I just can't bring myself to believe
I don't know what is truth anymore
Do you?

SweeTart

They say "there's one born every minute."
Your eyes are locked on the second hand, dear
with a handful of lollipops within your grasp
you have several in your back pocket
and leave a line of them trailing closely behind you
as you cheerfully skip along the walk.

Seductively twirling one between your lips
you dwindle each of them down
slowly
one at a time
leaving them an empty skeleton of themselves
not even having the decency to let go of the remains.
They are salivating puppy dogs,
you use their hanging tongues
as leashes
to keep them close
and lapping up every ounce
of your illusion
miserable fools
miserable empty . . . desperate fools
the whole lot.

Sad Little Puppy Dog (SweeTart Part 2)

What are you doing handing your leash
to an owner who doesn't even want you?

You know she doesn't want you,
she told you first hand.
But you'd happily lick her shoes for as long as she continues to let
you. Sad, sad puppy dog.
Your master is not the wonderful person you paint her to be.
You've got a cone around your head and you only see the illusion
she allows you to see.
She needs you for her own validation.
She needs you,
to feel powerful, attractive and popular.
You're a loyal pet who does and gives her what she wants at her
every beck and call.
All she has to do is tempt you, tease you with her body, her looks
and you're back on your knees and at her service, salivating at any
form of attention she pays you.
Even if it's cruel.
Move on,
my dear and sweet puppy.
There is someone out there who will actually value who you are,

take the time to pet you,

walk with you and occasionally give you a treat.

You're only hurting yourself by clinging onto this fantasy,

this cruel illusion.

Let go and find a master who's worth serving.

Excuses

OH MY GOD, SHUT UP!

Don't you ever stop whining?
Don't you ever stop complaining?
Don't you ever stop bitching about
all the downfalls and misfortunes of your life?

Crying about how things NEVER go the way you hope
how EVERYONE is out to get you
and how you are such a sad, hopeless, and helpless being.

Well, you know what?
EVERYONE has baggage
EVERYONE has pain
EVERYONE has had embarrassing
or traumatic,
scarring experiences
that makes them who they are today.

YOU are not the exception.
as much as you'd like to disagree with me,
you DO have a choice
just like everyone else does.

DON'T YOU DARE say that you're "stuck"
or that's "who I am" simply because it's the same routine you've
done for years.

Overgrown child
you'd rather whimper and moan
pointing fingers at others for your miserable life.

Well, honey, you can thank yourself for that
because you DO have the power to change your life
you just rather not get off your ass to do so!

You just keep going in a loop
doing the same things, over and over
dancing around the obvious action
that you keep avoiding.

I don't want to hear ANOTHER word of how

things come easier for other people

because you don't know where they come from

and you CERTAINLY don't know what they went through.

You want to know the BIG difference between you and others?

They made a CHOICE to take ACTION in their lives!

YOU don't!

Prisoner of Emotional War

HOW DARE YOU!
HOW DARE YOU blame her for him cheating!

"If she just stepped up and talked to him…."
You are his friend
but you don't know him on a relationship level.

Sure, she's mousy
but did you ever think of why she's so mousy?

Have you ever been with someone to where
EVERYTHING
about you was wrong
stupid
laughable
or even something to argue about?

Your thoughts

feelings

ideas

beliefs

your looks

or the way you carry yourself.

Every day your existence

is deemed repugnant to the one person who once

saw you as

"their whole world."

Every day

you wonder why they stick around just to insult you

when they could easily leave.

Every other night is a reason to be screamed at

stormed out on

or intimidated into submission.

You try to convince yourself that SOME part of that person

still cares and you stick around in hopes to find that person

who once treated you like a human being.

But every day stays the same.

He sticks around just to treat you like shit
to dash out the door when you want to talk
or gives you a "reason" to shut up.

You cannot reason with THAT
there is no "rational discussions" with THAT.

So don't you DARE blame her for his SEVERAL acts of
indiscretion.
Don't you ever think about it!

She was simply a prisoner of fear with him
and a brave soldier for us.

Encounter

Pull me close
embrace me tight
caress my skin
your fingertips cascading along sweet, silky softness
gaze into my eyes
hypnotize me
swallow me whole
leave my mind a void
as you make every cell within me come alive.

I want to feel your every breath
as the warmth of your lips meet mine
sweet, salty, slippery heat
every pore gasping in ecstasy and delight.

I experience every pound of your heart

through every inch of your body

flesh running hot

blood running high

as I transcend

awaken me

send me over the top

give me an out of body experience

don't question the circumstances

just follow your instincts

nobody will know

but you

and me.

The Brink

I'm there
about time
I've been aching for it
it's been begging to surface
to finally obey the moon
and let my baser instincts take hold.

I've been holding it back for far too long
taming it for an eternity
I can't hold it back any longer
I beg you not to push me
pleeeeaaase don't push me
I'm not afraid of you, my dear
I'm afraid of me
and what might happen to you
I might not be able to stop myself
so pleeeaaase lay off
I beg you.

As a matter of fact

on second thought

push me again

back me into a corner

I think I'm starting to like it

something stirring within me

powerful and strong

a sensation like tingles

in between my thighs

moving up into my stomach

and into my chest

burning like fire

and fueling my arms to do the unspeakable

my tongue is yearning

I crave again

as my eyes are blinded by a crimson fantasy

I only see you and no one else.

I want to tear, rip, snap

and hear the screaming moans of your agony

your whimpers

your muffled suffering

stifled by the very nectar you sustain on.

I stare deeply into the beauty

of the quivering mess before me

tingles increasing within me

as I reach intense satisfaction

completely intoxicated

lost in a trance

of ecstasy

covered in your nectar

I'm drenched

as I lift one hand up

and lick the length of it.

Living Dead Gurl (friend)

You're so breathtaking

stopped my heart from beating.

My eyes continue to stare as they fixate

Aren't I the perfect companion?

Quiet

sweet

still.

I'm just your type

my skin

so SO very fair

and cool to the touch

my lips

my hair

aching for warmth

not an eyelash flutters

as I remain quiet

attentive

ever so still

As I wait so patiently for you

I can wait an eternity

I can

And even longer still

Besides

you're the one who stopped my heart.

Zombie

Exhausted
she walks
unsteadily
dirt under her nails
grime on her face
clothes and hair
soiled, disheveled
lightning crashes
thunder roars
on a dark night
as she approaches a ragged wooden table.

Eyes blank and lifeless
she pulls her collar to the side
with one hand
as the other dives into the flesh of her chest
fingernails sinking deeper
as the tips reach and discover it's goal
grasping, her hand retreats
pulling out something dark, discolored
it quivers, suffocating for revival
as she places it on the table

and pulls out a rusty, jagged blade.

Slowly but surely

she slices away

piece by piece

emotionless, without a flinch

shredding away with the rust-serrated blade

mincing and ripping

as her eyes stare off into nowhere

as nowhere reflects in her eyes

she is empty

lifeless

nothing

but a shell.

Significant

We're a team
Aren't we?
Right?
Trust me
let's work together
fight our demons
our conflicts
side by side
let's face the world.

But where are you?
I am not your enemy
I am not your competition
Stop comparing me to you
walking away
running away.

Do you know how hard it is to fight a world alone?
When the reliable turns into an ostrich?
Who's willing to take a stand?
Who's willing to face the ugly, the dark, the scary, and
the pain?

Am I worth fighting for?

worth standing up for?

Who can fill those shoes to face the unknown with me?

Willing to shed blood & tears?

Who can absorb the blows with me?

Walk strong into our own hauntings

as we carve a path of our own

through this dark forest we call life

creating light with every step.

Who will be the one strong enough?

Who will be the one brave enough?

Who will have the will?

Pariah

Why are they all scared of me? Why do they run away?
Why, instead of embracing me, they cower . . . and stray?
A monster, a demon, disguised as an angel. Do I scare
you? Are you frightened? No. . . Liar. From a distance,
you like me, dream of and strive for me only to be sorely
disappointed and quiver at my movements.

What you see is merely an illusion, so stop trying. Stop. I
face reality, take a chance, take a stand. If you can say
that in confidence, please, take my hand. If you hesitate
then I understand. But no more charades, please please,
no more games. I can't take much more of the
dishonesty, guessing, anger, pain, shame. If you accept
me, for who/what I am, through and through . . . Let's
take on the world together "united". . . us two.

Worthless

"Do you know what it's doing to your lungs?

Your arteries?

Your thighs?

Your skin?

Your heart?

Your brain?

Your bones?

Your liver?

Do you realize how it hurts the earth, the air, the animals, the

water, and other people?"

Do the guilt trips end?

Ignorance is fucking bliss!

There's a negative to every side and we're all running scared.

If you're too fat, you're a terrible person.

If you're not smart, you're a terrible person.

If you're ugly, If you smell, if you don't have a degree or poor.

Don't believe in God, don't love the opposite sex.

We find the negative in everything.

We pick and prod our way to "perfection,"

an illusion.

People trying to find "balance" physically

when they don't realize that it isn't physical at all.

Robot Girlfriend

Perfect
always happy
always horny
very fit.

Oh so sexy
you love me
I'll always love you.
Whatever you want
whatever you need
I'll fulfill it
guaranteed
no questions asked
no thoughts or opinions.

That's what you want
always happy
never tears
always here to please
without fear.

I'm so perfect

oh so perfect

a hollow companion.

Just what you need.

Can I?

Can I?

Can I come to you when I'm in pain?

When I'm in need?

Can I talk to you about my favorite things?

Passions?

Beliefs?

Can I talk?

Can I feel?

Am I allowed?

Can I be me?

Can I? . . . . Can I?

I used to be explosive

expressive

dynamic

sultry

sensual

sexual

enticing

exciting

freeflowing

fun.

I used to be a lot more than what you see now
Can I be that way again?
Can you handle the real me?
Can you accept the real me?

Or would you rather a watered down and filtered
version of me?
Can I open up without censoring myself or being
censored?
Can I escape. . . . . . with you?

Ecstasy

In one quick move
I am severed from my senses
whispers in the darkness swirl and surround me
hissing in my ears as they hauntingly welcome me
flashes of memories, sounds, voices . . . faces
shutter in and out
as my breathing shallows, shortens, weakens
laboring.

My eyesight, hearing, smell, taste, touch, strength slowly fade
I can no longer hold myself against gravity
my body becoming one with the earth.
It is cold, as soon I will be
staring into nothingness
my eyes fixate and dilate
as pure crimson, undistilled life escapes my vessel soaking into the
soil beneath me.

I gasp

shuddering in my final moments

warmth leaves my body

I am one with the cold, cold Earth

I am one with the stillness of its nature

I am one.

12-2007

"Mon Cher" you called me.
We met only once,
you initiated me .

But don't leave me on this cold, dark ledge alone
guide me through these new dimensions
I already feel different from this world
Now I am truly isolated .

You tasted me.
I flow with you wherever you go
feel me as my emotions change.
The dizzying, breathless feeling as we replenished . . .
intoxicating.
My heart beats faster and faster as I slip under
my body weak from your hunger
I need you now
come to me.

Porcelain Steel

I'm your hollow, fragile, precious piece

locked up in your glass case

dust settles and weighs heavy on me

as I watch the world turn and evolve

you come in and dust me off

when you can't make out my face

or if I'm too close to the edge of my pedestal

about to shatter into a thousand pieces

denying the fact that I was the one who inched there in the first

place

pull me out every once and awhile

it's ok

I'm a lot more durable than I seem

talk to me

make me useful

make me feel

REAL.

Canvas

So many colors and shades on me

different hues from people painting me

each taking their turn to place me

sitting along Van Goghs, Rockwells, Botticellis, Monets

been SO many different things

pleasing to many eyes, except my own

I can fool them all but I can't fool myself.

Under all YOUR hard work is the real me

an "original" piece than a "master" piece.

So give me the fuckin' brush, bitch, and stand back

because my true colors are about to show

you may find some shades or colors not to your liking

but God help me if you try to "correct" them

my essence bleeding through and you wince saying, "I don't know

you."

That's right.

You never really knew me until right now, sweetie.

You were too busy placing me into categories

to realize that I don't fall into one

I hope you like what you see, baby, because once I'm finished, it's
not going to change this time .

Never Again
THIS paint won't come off,
It's infused within my fibers
Don't like it? Tough shit
I've got the brush now
And you have NO power
Just keep on walking to the art "of your choice"
I'm sure something down the hall would be more pleasing.

Fusion: United at Last

Hurling through nothingness,
a dark void,
a deep abyss
she blindly claws and extends herself to find no floors,
no walls
or surfaces.

But then,
a whisper,
her toes began to reach something.

As her weight became relevant,
her body pulls closer to this new surface.
She steadily stands herself upright,
adjusting to these new things,
weight and gravity.

The voice whispers again as she notices a glow in the abyss.
One foot after the other,
she slowly makes her way towards the small glow.
As she continues walking,

she notices the glow growing larger every time her name is
repeated.
She gets comfortable enough to move a little faster and begins to
jog. The calls become more frequent,
getting louder as she moves.
She stops abruptly as she sees the surging glow being blocked by
something.

Walls maybe?
She presses her fingertips against the dark surface,
letting them roam around as she walks along the length
of this obstacle.
Leaning as she courses along,
she suddenly feels nothing,
stumbling forward as she pummels herself into what
seems to be another wall in this darkness.
"Where's the voice?"

She continues to roam,
taking lefts and rights
and sometimes having to turn around completely.
The voice reverberates and echoes,
catching her by surprise.
The glow is bright now and along with it,

she can see a wall glowing in the same shade

and returning to black as it quiets.

She rushes for it as it repeats her name.

She now finds more walls lighting up in this shade.

Delighted to actually see the walls,

she moves faster towards this unknown voice,

calling louder,

beckoning her.

As she sees a very bright wall on the corner,

she pick up speed.

As she approaches the corner,

a woman slowly steps out from behind it,

stopping her dead in her tracks.

Trying to catch her breath,

she can't seem to take her eyes off her.

Stifled,

she falls to the floor looking up at this figure.

The woman is completely identical to her,

her face is calm,

confident

and reassuring.

Her stance is strong while her eyes are both loving and bold.

There is nothing "unsure" about this woman.

When compared,
her own face is twisted in confusion and uncertainty,
legs crumpled beneath her,
breath hasty as her eyes dart in different directions.

The woman holds out her hand and gently smiles.
Mesmerized as the letters R-O-E-A-U appear in her mind,
slowly she rises as she takes this woman's hand.
A whirlwind of emotion swells within her chest,
more than she can endure.
She closes her eyes and takes a deep breath
trying to
let it flow
through
her.

The woman wraps her arms around her as she speaks,
"You know who you are.
You know where you're going.

No one can stop you, but you.

No one can hurt you, unless you let them.

You've found me and I'll never leave."

As the woman dissolves,

her arms grows closer together;

slowly bringing her to hug herself.

The crimps and crinkles on her face start to smooth out

and disappear as she takes a gentle sigh.

A corner of her mouth draws up,

she gently opens her eyes as two voices escape her

throat in unison, "No one can come between us."

Roeau [Exp. 001]

Roeau . . . out . . . in a padded room . . .
wires running up into her head,
lifeless on the floor as a doctor peers through a one-way window.

On a desk lies a panel with several buttons
happiness
anger
sadness
fear
lust.

The man extends his hand to press "SADNESS".

Roeau begins to stir,
then moans and whimpers.
As her breath begins to shudder,
she pulls her knees into her chest and begins to rock while
pounding her head on the padded floor.
He releases the button.
Then . . . "LUST".
Roeau begins to breathe heavily and deeply.
She slowly rises to her feet while panting.

A frustrated look grows on her face.

All of a sudden,

both arms rise to her sides like the Christ crucified.

Her head moves side to side as if to dodge something.

Tears run down her cheeks as the "FEAR" button

begins to flicker.

Her breath hastily quickens.

The doctor leans into a small microphone and asks,

"Roeau, do you want to run?"

In desperation "YES!" she replies.

He continues. "Do you want to stay?"

"YES!" Roeau lustfully growls.

The "LUST" button is released as Roeau drops to the

floor,

breathless.

He reaches out for "ANGER" and hesitates,

then turns a switch which brings 2 guards in.

One man picks up Roeau's lifeless body and holds her

aside while the other man pulls up a patch of padding

from the center of the floor.

The doctor presses a button,

a metal chair rises in its place.

The two men seat her,

strap her in,

and leave the room.

The doctor reaches out,

once again,

and presses "ANGER".

Immediately,

Roeau's wrists pull tight against the restraints.

She begins to grit her teeth and growl,

spitting out obscenities,

intended violence,

and garbled gibberish.

Her heels twist and dig into the floor as her fingertips grip tight to
the arms of the chair.

In a quick motion,

Roeau frees her right hand from the restraint and helps undo her
left. She fights to free her ankles and snatches the wires out of her
head.

As she scrambles to her feet,

Roeau wrenches an arm off the metal chair.

She lets out a barbaric scream and flings it at the window.

She picks it up and throws it again,

cracking the reflective surface.

A shard falls from the frame.

She picks it up and jabs it at the window

growling,

snarling,

cursing

and threatening.

Gripping the shard tight,

she begins to slash herself as she continues to rant,

then sticks it into her shoulder

and drags it down the length of her arm as she lets out a hoarse,

bloodcurdling scream.

Roeau notices the guards are already in the room with her

and immediately raises the glass to her throat.

They slow down.

She giggles as she slowly drags the glass across her

throat.

She gasps.

The guards rush towards her.

Roeau points the shard at the men again and laughs,
revealing an unscathed throat.

One of them becomes brave and tries to tackle her.
They scuffle around and Roeau gets him from behind
with the shard to his neck.
She pants in a panic as her eyes dart from left to right.
Forcing him down to the floor,
she sits with him.

Tears run down her face as she slowly begins to realize
where she is and what she's doing.
Roeau drops the glass.
As the second guard moves in,
Roeau hastily grabs the man's head and twists it.
The man screams as he listens to multiple popping
noises within his throat.
Then . . . Silence.

Roeau collapses,
letting her face land on the pillowy white floor.
Her expression blank.
Eyes vacant.
Staring into nothingness.

Fear

What a hell of a world we live in
where we're constantly mind-fucked by propaganda
and the brain-washed society that follows it.
We know what we like
what we love
what we hate and fear.
And what turns us on.
Or do we?

Constantly being programmed since birth
steering us in one direction or another
herding us like sheep.
And we're happy little sheep, aren't we?

Flocking in any direction we're led to
not even realizing we're being led
by a built-in leash called our "senses" and "psyche."
Thinking it is how we have "chosen" to live.

We live life governed by the rules
made by someone before us.
Now every action,

every impulse,

every thought is held back

out of fear of shame,

embarrassment,

rejection

or infusing anger in others.

So afraid to "make a scene" or draw attention to

themselves.

All of a sudden it became "wrong" to do something

ridiculous,

pointless

or

illogical.

As if it were a crime to stand out.

Celebrities stand out.

They're eccentric,

they challenge the masses with their artistic expressions

and anger many with their strong messages.

But they are immediately accepted,

practically worshipped like gods.

What makes them so different?

Their money?

Their ability to do what the vast majority cannot?

Or that they do not care what others think and continue

forward with THEIR vision as extreme as it may be?

Isn't this the exact thing we ruled out?

Although we say it's okay to be different and unique

it's not outwardly practiced.

Living in a world of "dreaming" and not "doing"

where escaping into fantasy is so much simpler

than making it a reality.

In a bombarding,

overwhelming world

it's so much more convenient

to just tuck inside

and create a wonderful,

beautiful

and

perfect

world

of

your

own.

Instead of standing out,

speaking up and changing this dirtball

into the vision that plays in your mind.

What happened to this world?

Where are we now?

Who are we now?

Do we truly know?

Sour Settlers

Many sad, lonely, and angry people out there
who refuse to sort out the baggage of their past.

Out of fear of going after their dreams
they do the next thing and poke and prod
at the people who actually try and fight to stay hopeful and positive
as well as knocking at people who are actually successful.

They want to "watch the world burn"
those feelings didn't just come out of nowhere
one or many hurtful things led up to those feelings.

This doesn't justify anyone to stay miserable
but to learn to fight it to finally feel whole again
strong again in order to achieve what they really want.

If they had at least one person in their corner
cheering for them
and believing in them
they would realize that they are as strong today as they were
before all the scarring bullshit happened.

The only thing that changed within them is their perspective or point of view on things. There is no such thing as "this is the way it's always been so it's how it's going to continue to be."
No one is stuck unless they CHOOSE to be.

I chose to be for years
wasted a lot of my life being sour
going nowhere
getting worse and worse
wanting the worst for everyone
and myself.

If more people held onto what they want
fought to stay positive
and to believe in themselves
they'd find much more rewarding moments in their life.
They wouldn't be wasting their time spreading poison to others
trying to bring them down.

Sure, it's not going to be a perfect world
but less people would be bothered by the happiness or success of their neighbor
because they know they live a pretty awesome life as well.

A bigger percentage of people would be happy to see another happy

happy

for a change

rather than tiring themselves trying to prove how worthwhile they

truly are

or putting others down out of jealousy and insecurity.

What Happened?

What happened to….Passion?

That drive within us that urges us to do things without rhyme or
reason?

The want

the need

the instinct.

Everywhere I look I see people waiting to be TOLD what to do,

even when it comes to something they want.

They need to be instructed,

looking to someone else to give them "permission" to do anything.

I see people afraid…

to speak their mind or do what they feel,

to be one-hundred-percent themselves.

Rather than just letting go,

they need to organize a date, place, time and activity to "have fun."

What happened to us?

Did we lose our instinct?

Our independence?

Our individuality?

What happened to the carefree kid in all of us that yearns to play?

Today, it's all about fame or money,

who you know and where you go.

I have been seeing a lot of sheeple out there and I know you see them too.

Sheeple. Sheep people.

They graze from place to place, nibbling on whatever new patch of land they are led to.

BUT, as they are led, they are "bleating."

Complaining about the choices or actions that are being made and how their ideas would be MUCH better.

But they don't take the lead because that would involve
work and responsibility
people actually looking to them
NERVEWRACKING!

So they sit living under a decision
or order that someone else has made for them
and complain…..

Little Princess

Little princess sitting in her precious miniature box
adorned with decor and everything accustomed to her
liking.
Protected
controlled
safe
she rules behind these fragile and constrictive
boundaries.

But outside those walls lies so much more
more than she can handle
so she sits
remaining on her pedestal
waiting for the world to come to her

But oh no, baby bird
you must break out of your shell to spread your wings
and you must spread your wings in order to fly.
Yes, of course, within your capsule, you can enjoy "simulations" of
life but the world without holds so
much more, my dear.

How much further are you willing to go to keep your
surrealistic world intact?
What other stories have you concocted in your mind to
keep your "audience,"
the sea of mindless drones who follow your every word,
catering to your fantasy you call "reality?"

Your world
so small
stuffed with unnecessary items
waiting to crush you
within your own selfishness, stubbornness and fear.
You are capable of much more, my dear.
Break out, baby bird!
Spread your wings and fly!

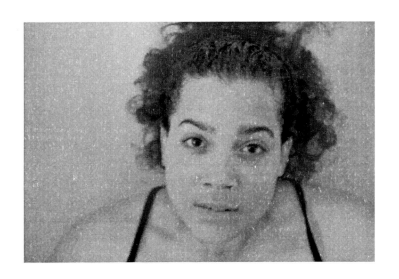

Your life is just that: YOUR LIFE.

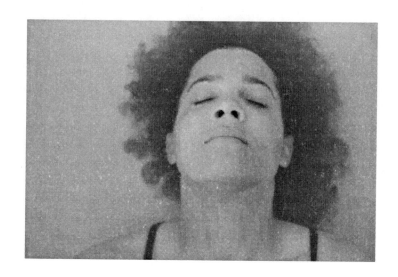

Speak up, Stand up, Take risks and Savor.

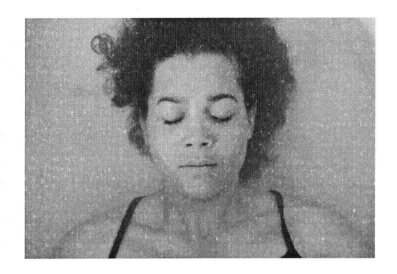

For the winding path before you is your breathtaking journey, only.

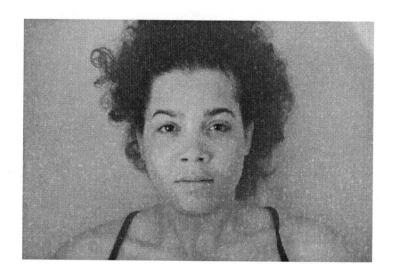

Many can show you the door. Only you can seize the chance to walk through it.